discovering nature

Weather

Sally Hewitt

Copper Beech Books
Brookfield, Connecticut

© Aladdin Books Ltd 1999

Designed and produced by
Aladdin Books Ltd
28 Percy Street
London W1P OLD

First published in the United States
in 1999 by
Copper Beech Books,
an imprint of
The Millbrook Press
2 Old New Milford Road
Brookfield, Connecticut 06804

Editor: Jon Richards

Consultant: Helen Taylor

Design: David West
CHILDREN'S BOOK DESIGN

Designer: Simon Morse

Photography: Roger Vlitos

Illustrators: Tony Kenyon, Stuart Squires – SGA
& Mike Atkinson

Printed in Belgium

**Library of Congress
Cataloging-in-Publication Data**
Hewitt, Sally
Weather / by Sally Hewitt.
p. cm. – (Discovering Nature)
Includes Index.
Summary: Introduces various topics related to weather,
including climate, winds, temperature, storms, and
more, using various simple activities.
ISBN 0-7613-0923-3 (lib. bdg.)
1. Weather Juvenile literature. [1. Weather]
I. Title. II. Series.
QC981.3.H48 1999   99-31619
551.5–dc21   CIP

1 3 5 4 2

Contents

Introduction

Hot sunshine, pouring rain, blustery winds, and snow are all different kinds of weather. You can have fun learning about the weather.

Find out how the seasons change as the earth moves around the sun, and watch out for signs of a storm. Take the temperature, make a wind detector, and keep a daily record of the weather where you live.

1 Look out for numbers like this. They will guide you through the step-by-step instructions for the projects and activities, making sure that you do things in the right order.

Further facts

Whenever you see this "nature spotters" sign, you will find interesting facts and information, such as the different shapes of clouds, to help you understand more about the weather.

Hints and tips

• Put the weather detectors you make where you can reach them safely. Anchor them securely so they don't blow over.

• When you go for a nature walk, take a waterproof coat and a sun hat, and be ready for all kinds of weather. Wear strong shoes and take a bag with a notebook and pencil and something to drink.

• Pay close attention to what is happening in the sky – what clouds can you see?, how hot is it? etc...

NEVER LOOK DIRECTLY AT THE SUN!

Wherever you see this sign, ask an adult to help you. Never use sharp tools or go exploring by yourself.

Get an adult to help you

This special warning sign indicates where you have to take extra care when doing the project. For example, you should never look straight at the sun. Its powerful rays can damage your eyes and may even cause blindness!

Climate

Some places are hot all year round, while others are cold or rainy. The weather a place has all year is called its climate. Make your own mini-climates and see how they affect how plants grow.

Hot, cold, dry, and wet

1 Collect four plastic tubs, some paper towels, and a pack of seeds that will grow quickly, such as grass or sprouts.

2 Put paper towels in the bottom of the tubs and sprinkle seeds over them. Now put the tubs in places to copy different climates.

SEED.

4 Put the last tub outside, but don't water it. Now see which of these four mini-climates is the best for growing seeds.

3 Put one of the tubs in the refrigerator. Here it will be cold, dry, and dark, just like a polar climate! Put two tubs on a warm, sunny windowsill. Water only one of these tubs and cover it with a lid.

All over the world

There are lots of different climates in the world. Which of these match the mini-climates you made?

Temperate climate
Temperate climates have warm summers, cool winters, and rain during any part of the year.

Desert climate
It hardly ever rains in a desert climate. Many deserts are very hot, but some, like the North and South poles, are very cold.

Rain forest
It rains nearly every day in a rain forest, and the air is always damp.

Seasons

The climate in some places can change from being hot one month to being cold in another. This is a change of seasons. It happens because the earth is tilted, as you will see from this project.

Tilting earth

1 You will need a friend and two balls, one for the sun and one for the earth. Paint one of them yellow to be the sun.

2 Paint a line around the middle of the other ball for the equator – an imaginary line around the earth.

3 Stick corks to the top and bottom for the poles. Now tilt the earth, and you will see that one half is closer to the sun. It will be summer here.

4 Now walk around the sun. Watch the half of the earth that starts off closer to the sun now become farther away. It is now winter in this half.

The seasons

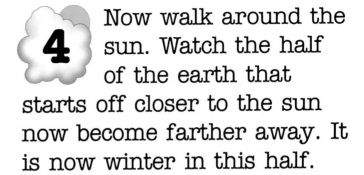

The changing seasons can bring about some dramatic changes to plants and animals.

Spring brings warmer weather after winter. Plants begin to grow, and baby animals are born.

Summer is the hottest time of the year. Trees and flowers are in full bloom.

Fall is colder. Leaves turn brown and start to fall from some trees.

Winter is the coldest season. Animals grow warm winter coats, and snow may fall.

During the summer, the arctic hare has a brown coat. In the winter, this changes to a white coat to help the hare hide in the snow.

Wind

The air around the earth is always moving, sometimes very quickly, causing storms. This moving air is called wind. Build your own detector to measure the strength of the wind.

Wind detector

1 For your wind detector, you will need a long stick, some thin string, tissue paper, writing paper, tinfoil, thin cardboard, thick cardboard, and a hole punch.

Get an adult to help you

2 Cut a strip from each piece of paper and foil. Punch a hole in one end of each strip. Tie the strips along the stick, with the lightest at the top and the heaviest at the bottom.

Tissue paper

Writing paper

Tinfoil

Thin cardboard

Thick cardboard

3 Take your wind detector outside to see how hard the wind is blowing. A breeze will move only the tissue paper. A strong wind will move the heavier cardboard.

The Beaufort Scale

This scale is used by weather experts to measure the strength of wind.

1 No wind	**2** Smoke moves
3 Leaves move	**4** Branches move
5 Crests in water	**6** Wind whistles
7 Trees bend	**8** It's hard to walk
9 Shingles blown off	**10** Trees uprooted

Air pressure

Even though you can't feel it, the air above you presses down on you all the time. This is called air pressure. Changes in air pressure usually bring changes in the weather.

Getting heavy

1 Air pressure is measured using a barometer. To make one, you will need a balloon, a glass jar, a drinking straw, a rubber band, a toothpick, scissors, and adhesive tape.

Get an adult to help you

2 Ask an adult to cut the end off the balloon and stretch it tightly over the opening of the jar. Then use the rubber band to hold the balloon firmly in place so it won't slip off.

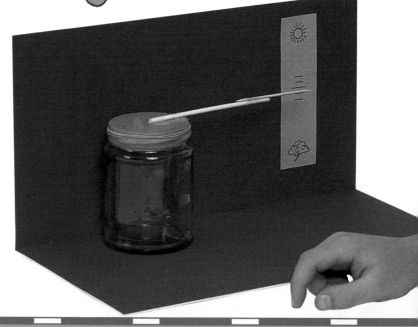

3 Tape the toothpick to one end of the straw. Tape the other end of the straw to the stretched balloon to make a pointer.

4 Because high pressure brings good weather and low pressure bad, draw the sun at the top of a rectangle of cardboard and a cloud at the bottom.

5 Attach the card behind the pointer. Watch your barometer over several days as the changes in air pressure affect the balloon, causing the pointer to rise or fall.

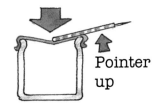

Pointer down

Pointer up

High pressure= Good weather

Low pressure= Bad weather

Barometers

You may have a barometer at home. Its needle shows the air pressure and the kind of weather you can expect.

Compare it with your homemade barometer to see how accurate your homemade one is.

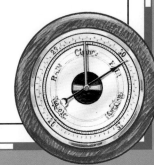

Water vapor

There are tiny droplets of water called water vapor in the air everywhere. Usually, you can't see it but when the air cools, this water vapor turns into larger drops of water and forms clouds.

Making clouds

1 You can make a cloud in a bottle. Fill a clear plastic bottle with hot water.

Get an adult to help you

2 Leave the hot water in the bottle for a few seconds. Now pour half of the water out and put an ice cube in the bottle's opening.

3 Watch as the ice cube cools the water vapor in the bottle and creates a misty cloud of water droplets.

 ## Clouds

Clouds come in lots of shapes and form at different heights. Their shapes and positions can tell us what weather we will have.

Cirrus clouds are high and wispy. They are a warning of bad weather.

White, fluffy **cumulus** clouds can turn into storm clouds.

Cumulonimbus are dark, towering storm clouds.

Stratus are layers of low clouds and can bring rain or snow.

Falling water

The water and ice particles that make up clouds (see pages 14-15) swirl around and bump into each other, becoming bigger. If they become heavy enough, they fall to the ground as rain, hail, or snow.

Collecting rain

Get an adult to help you

1 Make a rain gauge to see how much rain falls where you live. Ask an adult to cut the top off a clear plastic bottle.

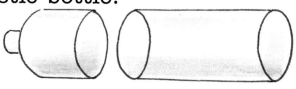

2 Turn the top of the bottle upside down and push it back inside the bottle. Tape over the sharp cut edges to make them smoother.

3 Put your rain gauge in an open place outside to catch the rain. Prop it up between four bricks to stop it from being blown over.

4 At the same time each day, pour any rain in your gauge into a measuring cup and check how much has fallen.

Snow and hail

Hail is made from ice crystals in the clouds. They clump together to form small balls of ice that fall to the ground.

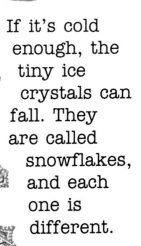

If it's cold enough, the tiny ice crystals can fall. They are called snowflakes, and each one is different.

Evaporation

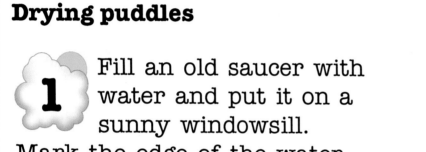

When the sun shines after a rainfall, puddles of water dry out. The water doesn't disappear, it becomes the gas called water vapor (see pages 14-15). When water does this, we call it evaporation.

Drying puddles

1 Fill an old saucer with water and put it on a sunny windowsill. Mark the edge of the water with a waterproof marker.

2 Mark the edge of the water in the saucer at the same time each day. The marks will show how quickly the water has evaporated into the air.

The water cycle

Water moves around between the land, sea, and sky in a cycle.

The sun heats up the water in oceans, rivers, lakes, and puddles and causes it to evaporate.

Water vapor in the air rises and cools. It turns into droplets of water and falls back to the ground. Rivers carry this water back to the sea, where it will evaporate again.

Water rains down

Water evaporates

Water vapor rises

Water flows downhill

Temperature

As the weather changes, you will notice that it gets warmer or colder outside. Temperature is how hot or cold something is, and you can measure it with a thermometer.

C F

Get an adult to help you

Sun and shade

1 You will need two thermometers. Inside their tubes is a liquid. When this liquid heats up, it gets bigger (expands) and rises up the glass tube.

2 Leave a thermometer in a sunny place. Make a note of the temperature that the liquid inside the thermometer is recording.

BE CAREFUL WITH THERMOMETERS – THE GLASS CAN BREAK!

Degrees

We measure temperature in degrees Fahrenheit, which can be written as °F.

Water boils at 212°F.

212°F

95°F outside feels very hot. Light summer clothes will help you feel cool.

95°F

Room temperature is 68°F, which feels comfortable and warm.

68°F

36°F outside feels cold. You will need to wear a warm coat and hat.

36°F

Water freezes at 32°F.

32°F

3 On the same day, leave a thermometer in a shady place. How does it feel in the shade? Is the temperature higher or lower than in the sun?

The sun

The sun's light and heat are bounced off, or reflected, by shiny things. As a result, they can be used to keep things cool. However, dark things take in heat and warm up, as you will see from this project.

Warm and cool

1 You need tinfoil, a black trash bag, two thermometers, modeling clay, adhesive tape, and two clear plastic bottles filled with cold water.

2 Cover one bottle in tinfoil and the other with the black plastic bag. Hold them in place with adhesive tape.

3 Put the thermometers into the bottles and hold them in place with modeling clay. Put the two bottles in the sun for about an hour and then check their temperature. Which bottle is warmer?

Sunglasses

Although the sun gives us heat and light, its rays are strong and can be harmful.

Sunglasses will protect your eyes from these rays in the summer.

NEVER LOOK DIRECTLY AT THE SUN!

Because snow reflects the sun, you may need sunglasses on a bright winter's day, too.

Storms

Storms are violent forms of weather, with strong winds (see pages 10-11), rain, lightning, and thunder. The best place to be during a storm is indoors. But you can still have fun experimenting with storms, even when you're inside.

Thunder and lightning

1 Thunder and lightning happen at the same time. However, because light travels faster than sound, we see the lightning before we hear the thunder. Measure the time between the flash of lightning and the crash of the thunder.

2 Figure out how far away the storm is: It takes five seconds for the sound of thunder to travel one mile. A ten second gap means the storm is two miles away.

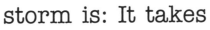

Whirling winds

Hurricanes are giant whirling storms, hundreds of miles across. They build up over warm, wet seas and cause a lot of damage along coastal areas.

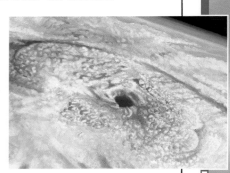

Tornadoes, or whirlwinds, are spirals of whirling air racing across land. They can pick up trucks, uproot trees, and destroy houses in their paths.

Pollution

The air around us may look clean, but it is full of dirt we can't see. Fumes from traffic, factories, and smoke all pollute the air around us, causing nasty weather, such as acid rain and smog.

Smoke gets in your eye

1 This is a way you can see pollution. Cut out one large and one small square of light colored cloth – old handkerchiefs will do.

Get an adult to help you

2 Glue the small square onto the large square of cloth. Glue it lightly, since you will need to pull it off later.

3 Hang the cloth up outside nearby, but not on, a busy road.

4 After at least a week, pull the small square away and see how clean the cloth is underneath! Pollution in the air has made the rest of the cloth dirty.

Smog and acid rain

Pollution in the air can make rain as acidic as lemon juice! Acid rain damages trees and even wears away stone buildings and statues.

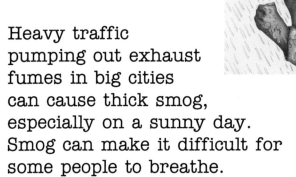

Heavy traffic pumping out exhaust fumes in big cities can cause thick smog, especially on a sunny day. Smog can make it difficult for some people to breathe.

Recording the weather

Use some of the projects in this book to create your own weather station. Keep a note of the measurements and see how they compare with the weather forecasts in newspapers or on television.

Keep a daily weather record

1 Hang a thermometer four feet above the ground in the shade. Read it at the same time each day.

2 Your rain gauge will tell you how wet or dry the weather has been.

3 High or low air pressure will help you to tell if the weather is going to be dry or wet.

4 Your wind detector will let you know if it is a good day for flying a kite!

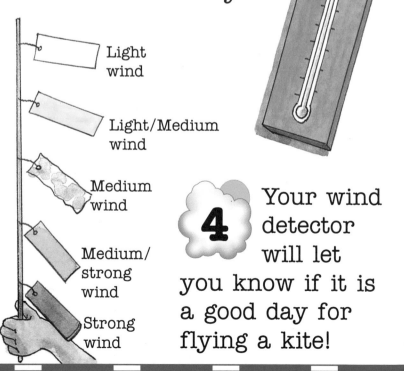

Light wind

Light/Medium wind

Medium wind

Medium/ strong wind

Strong wind

Weather maps

Weather forecasters use little pictures called symbols to make weather maps easy for us to read. Each symbol stands for a certain type of weather.

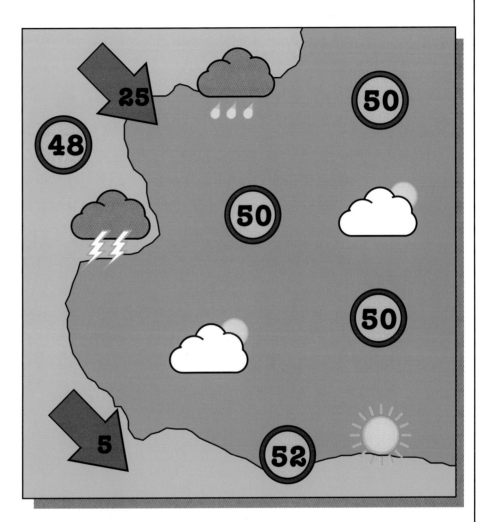

Dark storm clouds bringing thunder and lightning.

Clouds bringing rain or drizzle.

Clouds broken by patches of sunshine.

Clear skies and sunshine.

The arrow shows where the wind is coming from and how strong it is.

The number in the circle shows the temperature in degrees Fahrenheit.

Glossary

Air pressure

The air around and above you pushes down on you. This is called air pressure. Changes in air pressure usually bring changes in the weather.

Find out how air pressure affects the weather on pages 12-13.

Barometer

This is a device that measures air pressure and can be used to predict the weather.

Build your own barometer on pages 12-13.

Climate

The weather a region has throughout the year is called its climate.

Can you think of different types of climate? Turn to pages 6-7 to see some.

Clouds

Clouds are formed when invisible water vapor in the air cools and turns into visible droplets of water. There are many types of clouds and they are all linked to different types of weather.

Find out how you can make your own cloud and see some different types of cloud shapes and the weather they bring on pages 14-15.

Evaporation

When a puddle of water dries up, the water itself does not disappear – it evaporates. This means that it turns into a gas – water vapor.

You can measure how quickly a puddle of water evaporates in the project on pages 18-19.

Pollution
This can be caused when harmful chemicals are added to the environment. Pollution can cause nasty forms of weather such as acid rain and smog.

The project on pages 26-27 shows you just how dirty the air can be.

Seasons
These are yearly cycles of different types of weather. For example, winter is usually cold while summer is warm.

See what causes the seasons to change throughout the year on pages 8-9.

Storms
These are violent forms of weather, with strong winds and rain.

Turn to pages 24-25 to learn about different types of storms and how you can find out how far away a storm is just by using your watch.

Temperature
This is how warm or cold something is.

Measure the temperature with a thermometer on pages 20-21.

Water vapor
This is the gas form of water. Most of the time it is invisible, but you can see it when water vapor cools and forms clouds.

See this on pages 14-15.

Wind
Air that moves from one place to another is called wind. Winds can range from a gentle breeze to a tornado.

Measure the wind by building your own wind detector on pages 10-11.

Index

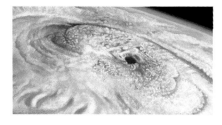